YOUR KNOWLEDGE HAS VALUE

- We will publish your bachelor's and master's thesis, essays and papers

- Your own eBook and book - sold worldwide in all relevant shops

- Earn money with each sale

Upload your text at www.GRIN.com and publish for free

Bibliographic information published by the German National Library:

The German National Library lists this publication in the National Bibliography; detailed bibliographic data are available on the Internet at http://dnb.dnb.de .

This book is copyright material and must not be copied, reproduced, transferred, distributed, leased, licensed or publicly performed or used in any way except as specifically permitted in writing by the publishers, as allowed under the terms and conditions under which it was purchased or as strictly permitted by applicable copyright law. Any unauthorized distribution or use of this text may be a direct infringement of the author s and publisher s rights and those responsible may be liable in law accordingly.

Imprint:

Copyright © 2016 GRIN Verlag
Print and binding: Books on Demand GmbH, Norderstedt Germany
ISBN: 9783668680869

This book at GRIN:

https://www.grin.com/document/419071

Samantha Bradley

Collecting Social Data. Methods of Social Research

GRIN Verlag

GRIN - Your knowledge has value

Since its foundation in 1998, GRIN has specialized in publishing academic texts by students, college teachers and other academics as e-book and printed book. The website www.grin.com is an ideal platform for presenting term papers, final papers, scientific essays, dissertations and specialist books.

Visit us on the internet:

http://www.grin.com/

http://www.facebook.com/grincom

http://www.twitter.com/grin_com

The Topic of this critical review is upon Gender, Place & Culture. Entitled Women students' perceptions of crime and safety: negotiating fear and risk in an English post-industrial landscape. The article explores the concerns of safety and fear of crime specifically on the perceptions of women students within a large town in the north east of England. The article is by Louise Wattis, Eileen Green and Jill Radford (2011).

Looking at the type/s of methodology used within this article we can see within the text that a qualitative approach was used (Wattis et al 2011). A qualitative approaches use language in collecting social data. It is more concerned with the participant's interpretations and understandings of their social world. (Jupp 2006) rather than gathering statistical and numerical data by quantitative approaches. Wattis et al have opted for a more in depth approach.

To record in-depth data semi-structured interviews have been used, this is allowing the researcher to guide the interviewee while also not completely limiting the respondent's responses the semi aspect of it allows for the researcher to guide the nature of the topics (Jupp 2006) in addition being able to use their own primary data/research to investigate and draw conclusions from furthermore being able to draw upon other data (secondary) to underpin the theories which they have uncovered. Or to inform us further of the understanding of the nature of crime and gender, broadly speaking. This research for the specific area has not been carried out before so is a good source of data to be able to analyse, explore and draw possible conclusions from. Furthermore, being able to compare to secondary data already collected on topics of which the researchers refer to in their paper.

Participant observation could perhaps have been a worthy methodological approach to use in gathering further information. In as much as the researcher would have been able to accompany the participants during their activities. The use of this approach would have allowed the researcher to be immersed within community and have been able to observe language and behaviour in order to gain insight to people's understandings (Jupp 2006).

Conceivably like piloting a questionnaire with the researcher sitting alongside the participant completing it and taking notes/ observing, (Foddy 1993) however here it is only observation to gather designing issues which may have occurred. The point being one would be able to gather further data which one may have not been able to with just the use of semi structured interviews.

Surveys are perhaps the most familiar method of social research and thought to be the most ' scientific' form of investigation using the quantitative approach ... where other methods of data produce unstructured data the survey produces a structured or systematic set of data this is taken from a very structured set of questions... the researcher begins by listing the variables with which he or she is concerned and then systematically collects information about each of these variables (Davidson and Layder 1994).

Nevertheless, as this article has a set of four components inter -related to their questions designed for semi structured interview which included;

- General attitudes towards the locality and local people;
- Fear experiences and factors contributing to fear, such as locations, social groups; types of victimisation; and also the role of 'safe' spaces;
- Awareness of how gender impacts upon experiences of space, fear and safety;
- Views on vulnerabilities connected to student identities; and where relevant, the exploration of other identities.

(Wattis et al 2011).

Primarily focused on the participant's views and observations the semi structured interview seems to be the logical choice here and to have worked for the purpose of the data they set out to collect although it could be argued that a mixture of other research methods could give a larger insight into the study. For example, the use of Ethnographic Research This type of involvement is required for unearthing good and reliable information about what is going on and why. (Davidson and Layder 1994). A criticism of this could be that the very fact a researcher is entering into their life's could compromise the scientific credibility of the research.

As Davidson and Layder describes some ethnographers have stressed the need for the researcher to avoid becoming over involved with people being studied, disturbing the natural setting and thereby compromising the scientific credibility of the research. Against This view, it has recently been argued that in order to truly grasp the lived experience of people from their point of view one has to enter into relationships with them (Davidson and Layder 1994).

Furthermore, it should be pointed out that with ethnography it is the researchers' observations of the participant which are recorded. Davidson and Layder suggested,

> Acting as a complete participant means the researcher has to adopt an almost passive demeanour, ... One problem with this role is that the required level of immersion and involvement in the activity its self may lead to neglect of the kind of analytic observation needed to develop an overview….
>
> (Davidson and Layder 1994).

Perhaps a point of contention is the idea that whilst collecting data with the semi structured interview technique allows the researcher to gather data from the respondents pertaining to their perceptions, it does not however account for wrongly perceived and recorded by the researcher or falsely given statements of accounts that participants may have had an encounter with the in the local community.

Furthermore, response bias could play a part in the viability of the data collected, here one is looking specifically at social class. There is another source of bias which is class-based what is more creates the 'education factor'. It is suggested from findings on victimisation surveys that the education level of a respondent is positively correlated with reported victimization, particularly from violent crime. In other words, the better educated you are the more likely you are to report being a victim of crime. (Coleman and Moynihan 1996). This perhaps could be a future question for research.

Wattis, Green and Radford tell us in the article the sample consisted of women from both middle-class (17 women) and working-class backgrounds (25 women) with class position established by women's family backgrounds. However, it is acknowledged that class categorisation can be problematic and this is especially the case when defining the class position of women (Wattis et al 2011).

Cross-sectional coding using the computer package Nvivo was used to organise and explore the data furthermore there is reference to Mason (1996, 108) as 'reading

through or beyond the data in some way' this meant that the data was also reflected on by examining what the data meant for both the researcher and the interviewees. Here the researchers used quotes of constant themes reflected from participants and some more of the more exceptional experiences of the respondents (Wattis et al 2011).

> Data were generated from the nodes using Nvivo and were read and analysed in this format. Dominant viewpoints and experiences were explored, as well as comparisons of differences and commonalities between different groups of women. (Wattis et al 2011).

Throughout this article the researchers make reference to a number of studies, theories and findings one such reference being;

> Despite de-industrialisation, the town retains a strong working-class identity originating from its heritage in heavy industry (Darnell and Evans 1995); a view corroborated by our research findings relating to how non-local students encountered the town.

These findings show us a theory from which they have taken which has emerged from the findings of their own study.

Could A more structured interview perhaps allowed for less bias but for this study and the specifics they wanted to find out there could have been interview bias within the questions asked. This study does not tell us what the specific questions asked were. One must also point out that you will always have interview bias and which this is unavoidable it is important to have reflexivity and acknowledge this within the study which Wattis et al have done throughout.

> Qualitative methods were used to gather in-depth data, which enabled interviewees to speak freely about their experiences (Reinharz 1992). Given the focus of the research, it was felt that quantitative methods would not be effective for obtaining data on women's fears and safety concerns. Indeed, despite the plethora of quantitative research on fear of crime, it has been argued that such methods do not provide any real insight into this issue (Walklate 2000; Lee 2008). That said, the limitations of qualitative research area acknowledged; one is aware that research only ever allows us a partial version of the social world (Miller and Glassner 1997).

A Further point to make is that semi- structured interviews allow the researcher to develop a good rapport with the participant and in fact with five of cases the interviews were undertaken with two participants present as they knew each other, one could say this could gather extra data for the reason that more topics could have arisen from hearing each other's view or it could have effected what the participant felt they could talk about in front of their friend. As Davidson and Layer point out interviews differ from ordinary conversation, they make the point that for someone who wishes to grasp the meanings that give form and content to social processes in an alien culture would not just administer a pre-designed, standardised set of questions and suggests establishing an excellent rapport by entering into a lengthy, in depth, unstructured interview would be.

> However, five of the interviews involved two interviewees – when respondents were friends and preferred to be interviewed together (Wattis et al 2011).

This article is published in A Journal of Feminist Geography specifically pertaining to Gender, Place & Culture, one could then determine the intended audience being for academics in addition anyone persons who would find this topic interesting, it is likely however to be favourable among social scientists in the broad term perhaps also more specifically for people studying feminism, gender and their experiences ontologically speaking within specific a society furthermore law and criminology academics. In other words;

> This article from an academic journal is intended for an audience well-educated in the field of social science. The author often uses technical language or "jargon" and assumes that the reader is already familiar with principles of social science. Moreover, researchers and specialists who are peers of the contributors (Research.moreheadstate.edu. 2016).

Specifically collecting social data. Within the context of gender place and society.

As this research study is asking for the participants experiences, views and opinions on crime one feels the need to mention The 'dark figure of crime' this articles sites statistics from the British Crime survey (BCS) and thus why I am mentioning the use of quantitative data collection that could be used to give insight into the dark figure, but as one understands the dark figure as it is set out it is understood that it may only portion ally give insight and the data may not necessarily be essay to determine the true nature of the answers given due to certain bias including the issues of ontology and constructionism regarding the nature of reality and how they view the social world through social interactions (Jupp 2006) for the specific participant/s

> The use of qualitative techniques offers the opportunity to make a distinct contribution by elucidating the contexts in which offending takes place and the meanings attached to such behaviour (Noaks and Wincup 2004).

Interwoven with the above issue is the data collected from the semi- structured interviews one here will mention possible problems associated with the type of data collected for example the problems surrounding the limitations of human memory, long term memory recall, short term memory, respondents will not always be able to provide the information the researchers are looking for due to the above factors and suggestions on studies done about long and short term memory (Foddy 1993:90-100).

A further point to mention that in comparison to questionnaires and being able to pilot your questions semi structured interviews offer the chance for the participant to ask any questions or talk about any aspect of the questions they would like to with the researcher.

Wider social issues pertaining to this paper are mentioned when the researchers talk about salience of gender, gender salience suggests that gender related self-concept has to be activated in order for ender identity to have a significant influence in a particular context…

(Patterson and Hogg 2016). Could this also be an issue of ethics due to the fact of gender being a social construct. Although the article has used British standard ethical guidelines both institutional and British Sociological Association pertaining to informed consent, confidentiality, and storage and access to research data.

> Informed consent was agreed upon prior to the interview and the participants were assured that they could end the interview at any time (Wattis et al).

A further point being that a number of the students were lesbian and they may have had a different experience specially with harassment and or sexual harassment depending on how male or female minded a person could be this relates to gender salience mentioned above. Crime is reportedly committed more by males than females but this is also a figure constructed by what may be data which some would say is not reliable, such as not including crimes which are hidden 'white collar' as these cannot be easily recorded. But from some social studies we can see how Lesbian females could harass other females just like males do.

Similarly, the ethnic minority group used only interviewed Asian respondents and we cannot see clearly which answers came from which groups within the study, we are only given a brief explanation of the more widely expressed views and some extreme views. Although one can ask to view the data collected for this study. We may then see a difference in not only gender but also race experience.

Other further parts to examine could be how the respondents may react or seemly be effected by our own biases in the way a question has been phrased.

Foddy (1993) Chapter 1- An initial statement of the problem. "factual questions sometimes elicit invalid answers"

'Palmer (cited by Deming 1944) found that, when respondents in a Philadelphia study were re- interviewed eight to ten days after in interview, 10 percent of the reported ages differed by one or more years between the interviews'

> likewise, Parry and Crossley (1950) reported that objective checks revealed that 5-17 percent of a random sample of over 900 Denver residents gave incorrect answers to a series of factual questions. The questions included whether or not the respondents had registered and voted in various elections, had contributed to the community chest; and possessed library cards and driving licences…
>
> if questions concerning such simple and apparently objective matters as 'age' elicit inaccurate data, one must wonder about the validity problems that might be associated with more threatening, more complex, or less well known issues.
>
> the relationship between what respondents say they do and what they actually do is not always very strong"

This seems to be what has been generally discovered for interview situations according to Foddy but he also points out that it could be possible there is a 'lack of clear conceptualisation of what is being measured' (Foddy 1993).

As one has established there are many ways in which the type of research used within this paper can help or hinder the researcher and will close with a reference to Pratt

> It is argued that leaving the matter of evaluation aside altogether, there is intrinsically more scope for disagreement in social study than there is in natural science, because support for any particular proposition or theory is so much harder to build. (Pratt 1978).

References

Allan, E., Abeyasekera, S. and Stern, R. (2016). *Writing up research: a statistical perspective*. 1st ed. [ebook] The University of Reading Statistical Services Centre: The University of Reading Statistical Services Centre. Available at: http://www.reading.ac.uk/ssc/resources/WritingUpResearchAStatisticalPerspective.pdf [Accessed 16 May 2016].

Britsoc.co.uk. (2016). *The British Sociological Association*. [online] Available at: http://www.britsoc.co.uk/the-bsa/equality/statement-of-ethical-practice.aspx [Accessed 16 May 2016].

Coleman, C. and Moynihan, J. (1996). *Understanding crime data*. Buckingham: Open University Press.

Corbetta, P. (2003). *Social Research : Theory, Methods and Techniques*. 1st ed. [ebook] sage. Available at: http://srmo.sagepub.com/view/social-research-theory-methods-and-techniques/SAGE.xml [Accessed 19 May 2016].

Foddy, W. (1993). *Constructing questions for interviews and questionnaires*. Cambridge, UK: Cambridge University Press.

Järviluoma, H., Moisala, P. and Vilkko, A. (2003). *Gender and Qualitative Methods*. 1st ed. [ebook] sage. Available at: http://srmo.sagepub.com/view/gender-and-qualitative-methods/SAGE.xml [Accessed 19 May 2016].

Jupp, V. (2006). *The SAGE dictionary of social research methods*. London: SAGE Publications.

Libguides.usc.edu. (2016). *8. The Discussion - Organizing Your Social Sciences Research Paper - Research Guides at University of Southern California*. [online] Available at: http://libguides.usc.edu/writingguide/discussion [Accessed 16 May 2016].

Mason, J. (2016). *Qualitative Researching*. 2nd ed. [ebook] London: Sage Publications. Available at: http://www.sxf.uevora.pt/wp-content/uploads/2013/03/Mason_2002.pdf [Accessed 16 May 2016].

Noaks, L. and Wincup, E. (2004). *Criminological research*. London: SAGE.

O'Connell Davidson, J. and Layder, D. (1994). *Methods, sex, and madness*. London: Routledge.

PATTERSON, C. and HOGG, M. (2016). *Gender Identity, Gender Salience and Symbolic Consumption by CLAUDINE E. PATTERSON AND MARGARET K. HOGG**. [online] Acrwebsite.org. Available at: http://www.acrwebsite.org/search/view-conference-proceedings.aspx?Id=12081 [Accessed 17 May 2016].

Pratt, V. (1978). *The philosophy of the social sciences*. London: Methuen.

Research.moreheadstate.edu. (2016). *Intended Audience - Distinctions Among Types of Periodicals - LibGuides at Morehead State University*. [online] Available at: http://research.moreheadstate.edu/c.php?g=106978&p=694271 [Accessed 16 May 2016].

you tube, (2016). *10 Hours of Walking in NYC as a Woman*. [image] Available at: https://www.youtube.com/watch?v=b1XGPvbWn0A [Accessed 19 May 2016].

Zamawe, F. (2015). The Implication of Using NVivo Software in Qualitative Data Analysis: Evidence-Based Reflections. *Malawi Medical Journal*, [online] 27(1), p.13. Available at: http://www.ncbi.nlm.nih.gov/pmc/articles/PMC4478399/ [Accessed 16 May 2016].

YOUR KNOWLEDGE HAS VALUE

- We will publish your bachelor's and master's thesis, essays and papers

- Your own eBook and book - sold worldwide in all relevant shops

- Earn money with each sale

Upload your text at www.GRIN.com
and publish for free